MUTINY ON THE BOUNTY

Two hundred years ago life on a sailing ship was not easy. You ate hard bread and bad meat. You worked night and day, often cold and wet and hungry. You saw no land for months and months. There were dangerous storms and many accidents; some ships never came home again.

In 1787 *HMS Bounty* leaves England and sails halfway round the world to Tahiti in the south seas. The captain of the ship is William Bligh, and his First Officer is Fletcher Christian. The *Bounty* is not a happy ship. Bligh is a hard man, and his officers and his men do not like him. They are angry and afraid – afraid of more long months at sea. It takes a year to sail home to England . . . a year of Captain Bligh.

They begin to talk quietly . . . Why not stay here in Tahiti, with its blue skies and its friendly people? Why do we need a captain? Why not put Captain Bligh in the ship's boat and send him home to England in that?

But the punishment for mutiny is death . . .

OXFORD BOOKWORMS LIBRARY
True Stories

Mutiny on the Bounty

Stage 1 (400 headwords)

Series Editor: Jennifer Bassett
Founder Editor: Tricia Hedge
Activities Editors: Jennifer Bassett and Alison Baxter

TIM VICARY

Mutiny on the Bounty

OXFORD UNIVERSITY PRESS

OXFORD
UNIVERSITY PRESS

Great Clarendon Street, Oxford OX2 6DP

Oxford University Press is a department of the University of Oxford.
It furthers the University's objective of excellence in research, scholarship,
and education by publishing worldwide in

Oxford New York

Auckland Cape Town Dar es Salaam Hong Kong Karachi
Kuala Lumpur Madrid Melbourne Mexico City Nairobi
New Delhi Shanghai Taipei Toronto

With offices in

Argentina Austria Brazil Chile Czech Republic France Greece
Guatemala Hungary Italy Japan Poland Portugal Singapore
South Korea Switzerland Thailand Turkey Ukraine Vietnam

OXFORD and OXFORD ENGLISH are registered trade marks of
Oxford University Press in the UK and in certain other countries

ISBN 978 0 19 478911 0

A complete recording of this Bookworms edition of
Mutiny on the Bounty is available on audio CD ISBN 978 0 19 478846 5

Typeset by Wyvern Typesetting Ltd, Bristol

Printed in China

ACKNOWLEDGEMENTS

Photographs used in this book are taken from the motion picture *The Bounty*,
starring Mel Gibson, Anthony Hopkins, and Sir Laurence Olivier, and appear
courtesy of Paradise Films Inc, copyright 1984. All rights reserved

Map on pp 28–29 by William Rowsell/The Garden Studio

Word count (main text): 5825 words

For more information on the Oxford Bookworms Library,
visit www.oup.com/bookworms

CONTENTS

1

From England to Tahiti

It was a cold day in December, 1787. There was a strong wind and a green sea. Three men and a boy stood on the deck of the little ship, *HMS Bounty*. Behind them, on the land, were some hills and small white houses. The ship moved slowly out to sea.

The boy, Peter Heywood, was fourteen years old. He was a young officer, and he was happy and excited.

'England looks very small, Mr Christian,' he said.

Fletcher Christian smiled at him. Christian was a tall young man with black hair and a long tired face. 'England *is* small,' he said. 'But we're going to some much smaller islands. Tahiti. The Friendly Islands. They're small, but they're very warm and beautiful.'

A sailor, John Adams, laughed. 'That's right, Mr Christian, sir,' he said. 'Good food, warm sun,

The ship moved slowly out to sea.

1

Fletcher Christian

blue skies – and hot, beautiful women, too! I want—'

'Be quiet, man!' someone shouted. Christian and Heywood looked behind them. They saw the captain, William Bligh. He was a small man with brown hair. Christian knew Bligh well; they were friends. But Bligh was a captain now, so things were different. The *Bounty* was his first ship, and it was very important to him.

'Don't talk about women on my ship, Adams!' he said angrily. 'Be quiet, and sail this ship! Do you hear?'

'Yes, sir,' said Adams quietly.

'Now, listen to me, Mr Christian. And you, too, Mr Heywood.' Bligh stood very near them, but he didn't speak quietly. All the sailors could hear him. 'I'm the captain of this ship – remember that! We're going thirty thousand kilometres through bad weather and very bad seas, and I don't want any accidents. You are officers, so you don't talk to sailors about women or drink, or anything! You must work hard, and your sailors must work hard, too. Do you understand me, Mr Christian?'

'Yes, sir,' said Christian. But he didn't look happy.

'Good. And you, Mr Heywood?'

'Yes, sir.' The boy looked at Bligh, afraid. Then Bligh smiled.

'Is this your first time at sea, boy?'

'Yes, sir.'

'Well, you must work hard, and listen to me. One day,

Captain William Bligh

perhaps, you can be a captain too. Would you like that?'

'Yes, sir, of course.' Peter Heywood smiled.

'Right then. Mr Christian! Look at those men there – they aren't working! Run and talk to them, quickly!'

Bligh smiled again at Heywood. 'In a happy ship, the men must work hard, but the officers must work harder. Do you understand, boy?'

The *Bounty* sailed south across the Atlantic. For ten days they were in a storm near Cape Horn, but they could not sail west because of the strong west wind. So they sailed east to South Africa, Tasmania, and Tahiti.

There were thirty-three sailors on the *Bounty*, and eleven

For ten days they were in a storm near Cape Horn.

5

officers. Bligh was the captain, Christian was his second officer. The ship was often wet and cold, but no one was ill. Once Bligh gave the sailors some apples, but they would not eat them because they were old and bad. Bligh was very angry.

'Damn you men!' he shouted. 'Apples are good for you! You eat them, I say!'

On 26 October 1788 the *Bounty* arrived at Tahiti. The islanders came to the ship in big canoes with food. The King of Tahiti, Otoo, was friendly. Bligh went to Otoo's house, and gave him things from the King of England.

'Thank you, Captain,' Otoo said. 'You are welcome here. I must give the King of England something, too. But he's a

The islanders came to the ship in big canoes.

*Bligh went to Otoo's house and gave him
things from the King of England.*

rich man. What would he like? Do you know?'

Bligh smiled. It was an important question. 'My King is
very rich, Otoo,' he said. 'But we don't have any breadfruit
trees in England. My King would like some, for his people in
Jamaica. Can I take some on my ship?'

Otoo laughed. 'Of course,' he said. 'That's easy! Take lots
of them. My people can help you.'

The *Bounty* stayed at Tahiti for five months, and by March
there were a thousand breadfruit trees on the ship. Tahitian
children played on the ship, and in the evenings the sailors
danced and sang with the women.

One morning, some sailors and Tahitian women took a
ship's boat to a different island. Bligh was very angry. When

the sailors came back, he put chains on their legs. Then he shouted at his officers and men. 'You men must stay away from these women!' he said. 'You must all listen to me, and work hard for me and the King!'

Some officers kept pigs on the ship. Sometimes Bligh took the pigs from his officers. 'I'm giving this food to the sailors,' he said. 'They need it, not you!'

April 4th was the *Bounty's* last day in Tahiti. The ship was full of food and people – Otoo and his family, all the sailors and their Tahitian friends. But nobody sang or danced. Everyone was quiet and sad.

Peter Heywood saw John Adams with a Tahitian woman. She cried, and he talked to her for the last time. Then she got into a canoe and went back to the island. Peter stood near him, sadly. The sun went down in the west.

'Mr Christian?' shouted Captain Bligh. 'Are all the Tahitians off the ship?'

'Yes, sir,' Christian answered.

'Good. Then we sail for Jamaica, and then back to old England!' He looked at Peter. 'Don't stand there, boy! Get to work! Look at all our beautiful breadfruit trees! King George is going to be very happy about them!'

2

Mutiny!

On the evening of 26th April Adams saw Bligh on deck. He looked angry, and stopped near Fletcher Christian.

'Mr Christian!' Bligh said. 'Where are my coconuts? I had fifty yesterday, and there are only twenty here now! Where are they? Do you know?'

'No, sir,' Christian said. 'I don't know. I never saw them. I didn't take them – you know that!'

Captain Bligh looked at his tall young officer and said nothing. Bligh and Christian were once friends, Adams remembered. But not now. Bligh was often angry; Christian was always worried, afraid.

'*Where are they? Do you know?' said Bligh.*

Bligh said: 'Mr Christian, you took my coconuts! I know you did! You're my second officer, but all you officers take my things! God damn you all!'

At four o'clock that morning, Adams saw Christian again. It was a quiet night, and the ship moved slowly through the water. Christian had a piece of wood with him, and a bag. His face was white in the moonlight. A young officer, George Stewart, talked to Christian.

'What are you doing, Mr Christian?' Stewart asked.

'I'm in hell,' Christian said. 'Bligh doesn't like me, or any of his officers! I must leave the ship!'

'Leave? What are you talking about? How?'

'I have some food in this bag, and wood, and I can swim,' Christian said. 'We're not far from the island of Tafua. Perhaps I can swim there.'

'Swim to Tafua? Of course you can't, man! Do you want to die?'

'It doesn't matter! I can't stay here with that man! I'm in *hell*, I tell you! Every day he shouts at me, and it takes a year to sail to England! I must leave the ship!'

'I understand,' Stewart said. 'Many of us are afraid of Bligh – we don't like him. But *you* must stay – you're our best officer. Listen to me, now . . .'

Bligh was in bed when the door opened. Christian came in,

with three sailors. It was still dark. Bligh opened his eyes. In the moonlight, he saw the gun in Christian's hand.

'What?' Bligh sat up. 'Get out, damn you! This is my—'

'Hold him!' Christian said. The sailors put Bligh's arms behind his back, and Christian tied them with a rope. 'Now, sir, come with us!'

They took Bligh out of his bed and up onto the deck. He wore a shirt, but no trousers or shoes. There were ten or twelve men there with guns and small swords. Christian held Bligh's hands with the rope, and Adams stood behind Bligh with a gun.

'What are you doing?' Bligh said angrily. 'Let me go at once! You're—'

'Be quiet,' Adams said. 'Listen to Mr Christian!'

'Hold him!' Christian said.

11

'But I'm the captain—'

'Not now. This is our ship now,' Christian said. 'Adams, put the launch in the water.'

The launch was a small boat, seven metres long. Adams put it in the water next to the ship. 'Right,' Christian said. 'Thank you, Adams. You stay with me.'

Christian looked at some other sailors. He didn't like them. 'You men!' he said. 'Get into that boat! Quickly now!'

'No!' Bligh shouted. 'All of you, stay on this ship! Help me, now!'

He began to run, but Christian held the rope and Adams held a knife to his neck. 'Do that again, Captain Bligh, and you're a dead man!' he said quietly.

At the front of the ship, Peter Heywood came up on deck. 'What's happening?' he asked. He was afraid.

'Be quiet, Peter,' Christian said. 'You stay there. Get into the launch, you men!' he shouted. 'I told you!'

Slowly, eighteen sailors got into the launch. Then Christian took Bligh to the side of the ship. 'Now you, Captain,' he said. 'Over the side.'

Two men carried Bligh over the side of the ship. Then the sailors threw some bread into the launch, with a barrel of water, a little meat, bottles of rum and wine, some rope and sails, and some of the captain's books.

'You see, we aren't going to kill you,' Christian said. 'You can live on that, for a week or two.'

'But why are you doing this, Christian?' Bligh shouted angrily. 'I'm your captain – and your friend!'

'No you're not! Not now!' Christian said. 'Don't you understand? I'm in hell, with you here on this ship!'

'You're going to be in hell all your life now, Christian, because of this!' Bligh said.

Bligh sat in the launch with eighteen men. Christian and

Bligh sat in the launch with eighteen men.

the sailors watched him from the back of the ship, then they opened a bottle of rum, and laughed.

'England is that way, Captain Bligh!' one of the sailors said. 'Thirty thousand kilometres to the north!'

'Forget England, my friend,' Adams said. 'I'm thinking about Tahiti, and those beautiful women! We're going to be happy now, on Tahiti with Mr Christian!'

Christian looked at Adams for a minute, but he didn't smile. His face, in the early morning sun, was white and cold. Then he looked at the launch, far away across the sea, with nineteen men in it.

'Tahiti, England, or the *Bounty* – it doesn't matter, John,' he said. 'I'm going to live and die in hell.'

3

In the launch

The launch was seven metres long, and there were nineteen men in it. Captain Bligh sat at the back of the launch, and looked at his men. The sides of the launch were only thirty centimetres above the sea.

'Mr Hall, look at our food, please,' Bligh said.

'Yes, sir.'

Bligh looked away, over the sea. The *Bounty* was very far away now, but there was a small island, Tafua, about twenty kilometres to the west.

After some minutes, Mr Hall, a young officer, said: 'Sir, we have 150 kilos of bread, two kilos of meat, six bottles of rum, and 126 litres of water, sir.'

'Is that all?' Bligh asked.

'We have a small sail, and some coats, sir,' Hall said. 'That's all.'

'Thank you, Mr Hall,' Bligh said. 'It's not much, but we're going to Tafua, so perhaps we can find some more food and water there.'

Bligh was afraid, but he didn't want them to see that. The men were quiet; they didn't look angry.

Next day they landed at Tafua. They found breadfruit, bananas, and coconuts, but no water. A lot of islanders came

Next day they landed at Tafua.

down to the sea. 'Where is your ship?' they asked.

'It sank,' Bligh said. 'All our friends are dead. We need food and water.'

The islanders laughed. It was not a friendly laugh. They talked quietly. More men came – soon there were nearly a hundred. They began to pick up stones.

'Get back into the boat!' Bligh said. 'Quickly, now.' But the islanders killed one man with stones. When the launch went out to sea, the islanders came after it in their canoes. They threw stones at the sailors.

'Throw the coats into the sea,' Bligh said. 'Quick!'

The islanders stopped and picked the coats out of the sea. Then the canoes went back to Tafua.

'We can't land on any islands, then,' Bligh said. 'Not without a big ship, and guns.' He looked at his men. They were quiet, and afraid. 'We must be very careful with our food,' he said. 'Every man can have a small piece of bread and coconut today, and a cup of water. That's all. When it's cold we can have some rum. But don't worry. Remember, I'm your captain. Listen to me, and we can stay alive.'

'Yes, sir.'

Then the youngest, a boy called Robert Tinkler, said: 'I want to go home.'

Bligh looked at him, and for a minute the boy was afraid, because Bligh was often angry. Then he saw a small, cold smile on Bligh's face. 'To England, Robert?'

'Yes, sir.'

'Well, that's about thirty thousand kilometres away. So first, let's find Timor. That's much nearer. There are Dutch ships there; they can take us home.'

'Yes, sir.' The boy looked happier. 'How far is it to Timor, sir?'

For a minute Bligh didn't answer. He looked away, over the cold green sea. The wind was stronger now, and the sky was dark. 'Oh, not far,' he said slowly. 'Only about seven thousand kilometres.'

Next morning the wind got stronger and stronger, and the

The wind was stronger now.

launch went up and down over big green waves. Everyone was wet, and white water came into the launch. The sailors used the empty coconuts to throw the water back into the sea. At midday they ate five small coconuts and drank some rum, and they ate some wet breadfruit in the evening. The wind and waves were strong all night, so no one could sleep.

Next day, the bread was wet, but they didn't throw it away. In the afternoon it rained, and they caught the water in cups and coconuts. But it rained all night, so everyone was cold and wet. The launch was small, so they could not all sleep. Most men sat up all night.

On 8th May it was sunny. The men took off their wet shirts

and trousers. Bligh gave them some rum, coconut milk, and eighty grams of bread. Often he talked about New Guinea, Australia, and Timor.

There were storms for the next two weeks. Sometimes they saw the sun for an hour, but every day it rained. Big green waves threw white water into the launch. They were always wet, tired, and hungry. Three times they saw islands, but they didn't go near them. They ate bad bread and old meat, but they had lots of rain water to drink. When they were very wet, Bligh gave his men some rum. No one could sleep for more than one or two hours.

But every hour, Bligh held a long rope over the side. The rope had knots in it. The men watched carefully. The knots went behind the launch, and Bligh looked at his watch. 'We're going quickly today,' Bligh told them, and wrote in a little book.

'We're going about one hundred and sixty kilometres every day,' he told his men. 'But we can't always sail west, because of the wind. So, I'm sorry, but today we can only have forty grams of bread.'

'Bad bread, too,' said one man, Purcell.

'Yes, but it keeps us alive,' Bligh answered angrily. Then he laughed. 'Look – up there!' he said.

There was a bird on the front of the launch. Its small yellow eye looked at them. Carefully, two sailors opened their hands, very slowly. The bird didn't move. One man put his hand on it. The bird moved away. But at the same time, his friend caught the bird's feet, and killed it.

The sailors laughed and shouted. It was only a very small black and white bird, but it was *food!* Good food!

'I caught it!' the first sailor said.

'No, you didn't!' the other man said. 'I did!'

'Be quiet!' Bligh said. 'Give it to me.' He cut the bird with his knife, and caught its red blood in a cup. The men drank the blood. Then Bligh cut the bird into eighteen pieces and put them in front of him.

'Right,' he said. 'Fryer, sit here, with your back to the bird. Now, I have one piece of the bird in my hand.' He held up a piece of its leg. 'Tell me, Fryer, who shall have this?'

'Ledward,' Fryer said.

'All right.' Bligh gave the piece to Ledward, and picked up a second piece. 'And who shall have this?'

'Hall.'

'All right.' No one was angry, because Fryer couldn't see the pieces. Everyone watched. Bligh picked up the bird's head and feet. 'Who shall have this?' he asked.

'Bligh,' Fryer answered. Everyone laughed, and Bligh looked at the head and feet sadly. 'Oh well,' he said. 'I know it's good for me.' Slowly, he began to eat them.

That evening, they caught a bigger bird, and ate that too. Next day they caught one more. Everyone was happy.

'Why are all these birds here?' the boy Robert asked.

Bligh smiled. 'Because we are near land,' he said.

On 28th May, at midnight, they saw white water in front of them.

'The Barrier Reef,' Bligh said. 'A line of rocks underwater. We must be careful – ships often sink here! Take down the sail, and move slowly. We must find a way through!'

They sailed slowly near the white angry water. Then, after four hours, they found a way through. Behind the Barrier Reef, the sea was blue and quiet. They sailed quietly to a small island.

They could sleep on the island, and walk about. They

They sailed quietly to a small island.

began to look stronger. But they were two thousand kilometres from Timor, so they could not stay long. After six days they went to sea again – west, towards Timor. The sun was very hot, and two men were ill. Bligh gave them some rum, and the blood of birds. 'But they can't live much longer in a little boat like this,' he thought. 'We're all tired and hungry – someone is going to die soon.'

But it was not far now. Every hour Bligh held the rope over the side, and wrote in his little book. He watched the sun and the sea and the sky. And then, on 11th June, Bligh said: 'You cannot see it, but south of us, there's a big island called Timor.'

They laughed and smiled and sang. Next day, they saw the island – green trees and hills. Two days later, they came to a town called Caupang. There were some Dutch sailors by the sea. Bligh and his men walked up to them.

'Who are you?' a Dutch officer asked. 'You look hungry, and ill. Where are you from?'

'I'm Captain William Bligh, of the English ship *HMS Bounty*. These men are English sailors. We left Tafua forty-one days ago.'

'Tafua?' the Dutch officer asked. 'Where is that?'

'It is a small island, about seven thousand kilometres away. We came in that small launch.'

'My God! Forty-one days – in that!' The Dutchman looked at the launch, and for a minute he said nothing. Then he asked: 'Did many of you die?'

Bligh smiled. 'Oh no. Only one, and the islanders on Tafua killed him. Seventeen men left Tafua with me, and seventeen men are here now. Alive.'

'I'm Captain William Bligh, of the English ship HMS Bounty.'

4

The Pandora

They sent Captain Edwards, in the Pandora, *to Tahiti.*

On 14th March 1790, Bligh and his men arrived in England. When he told the story of the mutiny, English people were very angry. They sent Captain Edwards, in the *Pandora*, to Tahiti.

On 23rd March 1791, the *Pandora* arrived in Tahiti. Captain Edwards and his men looked carefully at the island. They could see a lot of trees and small houses, but no English ship. Then, a small canoe came out to the *Pandora*. The three men in the canoe shouted and smiled.

'I think they're Englishmen, sir,' a sailor said.

'All right,' Captain Edwards said. 'They can come on the ship. Perhaps they can tell us something.'

The three men were brown and strong, but they wore English sailors' hats and trousers. One of them – a boy, about eighteen years old – smiled at Edwards.

'Good morning, sir! My name is Peter Heywood – I'm a young officer from the *Bounty*. This is Mr Stewart, and Joseph Coleman, a sailor.'

'Yes, I see,' said Edwards. 'Three of you? Where are your friends? Where is Mr Christian and the *Bounty*?'

Heywood looked worried. 'Mr Christian? He sailed away in the *Bounty*, sir, a year ago, I think. But we didn't go with them. We waited – for you. We aren't afraid.'

'I see,' Edwards said. He looked at them carefully. 'All right, then. Tell me your story. What happened, after Christian put Captain Bligh in the launch?'

'Well, sir,' Heywood said. 'We threw the breadfruit trees into the sea, and sailed here, to Tahiti. Otoo, the King of Tahiti, was good to us, and a lot of men wanted to stay here. But Mr Christian was afraid. "We can't stay here," he said, "because a ship is going to come from England." So Otoo gave us a lot of pigs, and goats and food, and we sailed to a different island, Toobouai. Some islanders from Tahiti came with us – eight men, nine women, and seven boys. But the people of Tooboaui didn't like us, and some of us didn't like Mr Christian. So Mr Christian sailed the *Bounty* back to Tahiti, and left sixteen of us here.'

'And then?' Captain Edwards was excited. 'What did Mr Christian do?' he asked.

'He sailed away in the *Bounty*, sir.'

'I see. And how many men went with him?'

'Nine sailors, I think, sir. But they took seven Tahitian men and twelve women, too.'

'I see,' Edwards said. He looked at them angrily. 'Sixteen men stayed on Tahiti, and three of you are here. So where are the other thirteen? Are they waiting for me, too, on the island?'

'Er . . . well, yes, sir . . . I mean . . .' Peter Heywood stopped. He was worried and afraid.

'They *were* here, but they aren't here now,' said George Stewart quickly. He put his hand on Peter Heywood's arm. 'They sailed away too.'

'Oh, did they?' Captain Edwards asked. 'When?'

Heywood and Stewart both spoke at once.

'Four days . . .'

'Two weeks . . .'

'. . . ago, sir,' they said. Then they stopped.

Edwards watched them. 'I see,' he said slowly. 'First you are in a mutiny, and now you tell me things that are not true! Sailor!'

'Yes, sir,' one of the *Pandora*'s sailors answered.

'Put these three men in chains. They are prisoners.'

'But sir!' Peter Heywood said. 'We didn't run away! We came to tell you our story. And Mr Stewart has a wife!'

'A *wife*?' Captain Edwards laughed. 'Is she at home in England?'

'No, sir. Here,' Mr Stewart answered. 'She's a Tahitian

26

woman. Her name is Peggy – Mrs Peggy Stewart. And we have a daughter.'

Edwards laughed again. 'A Tahitian woman! I'm sorry for her! But don't worry. She can come on the ship and see you in your new prison. Look behind you. We have a wonderful prison for you and your friends. Look!'

The three sailors looked behind them. On the deck of the *Pandora* was a wooden box, about two metres high and four metres long. It had a small door, but no windows. The *Pandora*'s sailors put the prisoners in the box, with chains on their arms and legs. Captain Edwards laughed.

'There! Are you happy now? You can stay there, all the way to England!'

'But . . . my wife! My little daughter!' Stewart said. The door closed in his face. '*We* didn't put Bligh in the launch – Christian did! We came to tell you everything!'

Edwards laughed, and Peter Heywood said nothing.

Captain Edwards caught eleven more men, and put them in the *Pandora*'s box, too. Their Tahitian wives and children came onto the *Pandora* and cried, but Captain Edwards didn't open the door. For three months, the *Pandora* sailed to different islands, and the prisoners stayed in the box. But Edwards couldn't find Christian or the *Bounty,* and so he began to sail home.

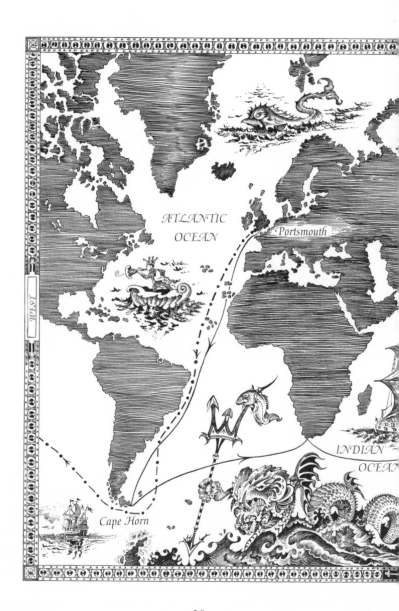

ATLANTIC
OCEAN

Portsmouth

WEST

INDIAN
OCEAN

Cape Horn

THE BOUNTY

Bligh's launch and the Pandora

E

S

PACIFIC
OCEAN

EAST

New Guinea

Timor

Tahiti

Great
Barrier
Reef

Tafua

Toobouai

Pitcairn

Australia

LEGEND
———— Bounty under Bligh
•••••••• Bounty under Christian
- - - - Bligh's launch
-·-·-· Pandora

Near Australia, the *Pandora* hit the Barrier Reef. Water came into the ship, and the sailors couldn't stop it. After twelve hours, Captain Edwards said: 'We must leave the ship! Get into the boats, men!'

The prisoners could hear the noise outside, and water came in through the door. Captain Edwards took three prisoners out, but then he closed the door.

'What about us?' Peter Heywood shouted. 'Please, Captain, open the door! Why are you leaving us in here?'

'Be quiet, boy!' said Captain Edwards. 'We're working hard now – the ship is sinking!'

'But we're going to die – we can't move!' George Stewart shouted. 'Open the door!'

But Edwards closed the door, and no one helped them. Outside, the first sailors got into the boats, and rowed away. Inside the box, the prisoners hit the walls, and shouted. But they couldn't move, because of the chains.

After an hour, a sailor opened the door and helped them out of their chains. But there was very little time. All of them got their legs free, but some couldn't get their arms free. Peter Heywood was nearly the last man to get out. In the sea, he held on to some wood. He saw George Stewart and four other prisoners. They couldn't swim, because of the chains on their arms.

'Help me, Peter!' Stewart called. But the sea took Stewart away. Peter Heywood never saw his friend again.

Peter Heywood landed on a small island with some prisoners, Captain Edwards and the *Pandora*'s sailors. They had four boats, but only one small barrel of water and some bread. Like Captain Bligh, they sailed to the Dutch island of Timor. Then a Dutch ship took them to England. They arrived on 19th June 1792.

Peter Heywood looked across the water at the green hills and small houses. 'Home,' he said quietly to a Dutch sailor. 'England is very beautiful, you know. I left here five years ago!'

'Are you going to see your family?' the Dutchman asked.

'Not yet,' Peter answered. 'I must go to my trial first. And the punishment for mutiny, you know . . .'

He stopped. The wind moved his brown hair. The Dutchman put a hand on his arm.

'I know, Peter,' he said sadly. 'The punishment for mutiny . . . is death.'

5

Death, life, and Thursday

There were nine captains at the trial. Peter Heywood stood in front of them, and talked about the night of the mutiny.

'It was four years ago,' he said. 'I was a young officer, fifteen years old. When I came up on deck, Captain Bligh was Mr Christian's prisoner. How could I help him? I didn't have a sword or a gun. Mr Christian put Captain Bligh and eighteen men into the launch.'

There were nine captains at the trial.

32

One of the nine captains asked: 'Did you try to help Captain Bligh, Mr Heywood?'

'No, sir. I couldn't. Christian and his men had swords and guns . . . I had nothing.'

A different captain asked: 'Did Mr Christian do the right thing, then? What do you think?'

'No sir, of course not!'

'But you didn't get into the launch with Captain Bligh. Why not?'

'I couldn't, sir! It was full. There were nineteen men in it. It nearly sank without me.'

'Did you say anything to Captain Bligh?'

'Er . . . no, sir, I didn't. Some men did, but not me.'

'So, Mr Heywood, you were an officer on the *Bounty*, and you saw this mutiny, but you did nothing. You just stood, and watched. Is that right?'

'Er. . . yes, sir.' Peter Heywood was afraid now. 'I was . . . very young then, sir.'

'You were an officer. An officer must always help his captain. Wait there.' The nine captains walked out of the room.

Peter waited for a long time. His mother and sister were with him, but he felt afraid. Then the captains came back, and the oldest captain said: 'Peter Heywood, because you did not help Captain Bligh, we say you helped the mutiny. And there is only one punishment for mutiny. Death. Do you understand?'

Peter's face was white and he felt ill. But he said quietly: 'Yes, sir. I understand.'

Two days later he saw the oldest captain again. There was a small, cold smile on his face. 'Mr Heywood, I have a letter from the King. The older sailors must die, but because you were a young boy on the *Bounty,* the King says you can live. You can go, Mr Heywood. You are a free man.'

'Oh, sir! Thank you. Thank you very much.'

Peter Heywood lived for many years. Twenty years later, he was a captain of a ship, like Captain Bligh.

Captain Bligh went back to Tahiti, and took some more breadfruit trees to Jamaica. After that, he sailed many more ships. He was an important man. He died in 1817.

But what happened to the *Bounty,* and Fletcher Christian? For years, no one knew. Then, twenty years after the mutiny, in 1809, an American ship, the *Topaz,* visited a small island called Pitcairn. When the captain of the *Topaz* came home, he had an interesting story. And five years after that, in 1814, two British ships – the *Briton* and the *Tagus* – arrived.

Pitcairn was a small island with nowhere good for ships to land. But a canoe came out through the white water to the British ships. The men from the canoe came onto the *Briton* and looked for the captain, Sir Thomas Staines.

'Good afternoon,' he said. 'Who are you?'

Two days later he saw the oldest captain again.

A tall young man answered: 'I'm Thursday.'

'I'm sorry,' Captain Staines said. 'What did you say?'

'My name is Thursday,' answered the young man. 'Thursday October Christian. I live on this island. You are welcome here. Would you like to come to my village, and eat with us? Mr Adams would like to see you.'

'Well, thank you very much,' said Captain Staines. 'And Captain Pipon, from the *Tagus* – can he come too?'

'Of course,' said Thursday. 'He is welcome.'

The two captains got into the canoe, and Thursday and his friends took it through big green and white waves to the island. Near the beach was a small village.

'How many people live here?' Captain Staines asked.

'About forty,' said Thursday. 'Here is our king, John Adams.'

An old man with white hair came towards the two captains. He wore trousers and an English sailor's shirt. 'Good afternoon,' he said. 'My name is John Adams, of *HMS Bounty*. Welcome to Pitcairn Island.'

Some old women gave the captains wonderful food, and John Adams told them his story.

'When the *Bounty* left Tahiti, Christian was very worried. "A ship is going to come from England," he said. "They want to kill me. They must never find us." So when we landed here, we took all the pigs and goats, and burned the *Bounty*. We stood by the sea and watched. Then we made our village. But

Christian was always worried and afraid, and it was difficult to live here. The Tahitian men didn't like the English sailors. There were ten English men, seven Tahitian men, and twelve Tahitian women. When Christian took the wife of one of the Tahitian men, the Tahitian man killed him. Then the Tahitian men killed most of the English men – they nearly killed me! But the women stopped them – the women killed the Tahitian men! After that, there was one man alive on the island – me! But there were nine women, and some small children – this young man, Thursday, is Fletcher Christian's son.'

'Oh, I see!' said Captain Staines. 'So . . . you were alone here, with nine wives!'

We stood by the sea and watched.

37

John Adams smiled. He looked a tired but happy man. The old women near him smiled too. 'Well, yes, sir,' he said. 'But I'm a good husband to them, and a good father to all these children. And of course, now that these boys are men, they have wives too . . .'

'Do you all speak English?' Captain Pipon asked.

'Yes, sir. English and Tahitian too. We have our pigs and goats and coconut trees, and we think about God every day, sir.'

'You are very happy,' Captain Staines said.

'We are, sir,' John Adams said. 'All of us. But . . .' He stood up slowly. 'I know why you are here. You are going to take me to England with you. I must die there.'

Captain Staines looked at him. The Pitcairn islanders looked very sad, and some of the women began to cry.

'What do you mean, man?' Captain Staines asked.

'Well, Captain, I was in the mutiny against Captain Bligh. It was a long time ago, but I did it. I must take my punishment.'

'But . . . my God!' Captain Staines looked at Captain Pipon. 'Of course the man is right,' he said. 'But . . . we can't do this. You're an old man, Mr Adams, and you are happy here. Your wives and children need you. It was twenty years ago, man! People in England don't talk about the *Bounty* today. And Fletcher Christian is dead!'

'*He* is dead, but I'm not,' John Adams said. 'I helped him, and I'm here, now, in front of you.'

'And this is your home,' Captain Staines said. 'You are an old man. You must die here – not in England. Sit down, Mr Adams. Let's finish this wonderful food.'

'All right, Captain,' John Adams said. 'And . . . thank you.' He sat down, and the Pitcairn islanders smiled.

'Tell me about Bligh,' Captain Staines said. 'He's an important man now, you know. But most people like him. Why were you all angry with him?'

Adams thought for a minute. He looked up at the trees over his village, and at the smiling faces of his wives and children. 'Bligh,' he said. 'Well, he was a good sailor, of course. We were angry with him, but I can't remember why. It's a very long time ago . . .'

❖

GLOSSARY

barrel a big 'bottle' for wine, water, beer, etc.

bird an animal which flies

breadfruit a big fruit, like an apple

blood the red liquid in a person's body

burn to make a fire

canoe a small wooden boat

captain the most important officer on a ship

catch (past tense **caught**) to get something with your hands

chain a metal rope

coconut a big brown hard fruit; it has sweet white food and 'milk' inside

cut to open something with a knife

dance to move your body to music

damn a bad word; people say this when they are angry

death the end of life

deck the door of a ship

food the things we eat

full something is full when you cannot put any more into it

goat a small animal, like a sheep

God the 'person' (in the Christian religion) who made the world and knows everything

gun a thing that shoots out bullets to kill or hurt people or animals

hard very difficult

hell some people believe that bad people go to hell when they die

hold (past tense **held**) to have something in your hands

island a piece of land with water all round it

keep (past tense **kept**)   to have something and not give it to
   another person

king   the most important man in a country

knot   a place where you tie two pieces of rope together

land *(n)*   the part of the earth that is not the sea

land *(v)*   to come out of a boat onto the land

launch   a small boat

mutiny   a mutiny happens when sailors fight the captain (and
   sometimes kill him) and then take control of the ship

officer   a man (more important than a sailor) who works for the
   ship's captain

pig   a small animal

pick up   to take something into your hand

prisoners   people in a prison (a place for bad people)

punishment   paying money, going to prison, death, etc. (what
   happens to people when they do bad things)

rope   very thick, strong string

rum   a very strong drink, like whisky

sad   not happy

sail *(n)*   a large cloth on a ship, to catch the wind

sail *(v)*   to make a ship move

shout   to speak very, very loudly

sink (past tense **sank**)   to go down under water

sir   a polite word for a man

stone   a small piece of rock (the hard stuff in the ground)

storm   very bad weather: a lot of rain and wind

strong   a strong person can carry heavy things, does not get
   tired easily, etc.

swim   to move in water

sword   a long, big knife

throw (past tense **threw**)   to make something go quickly
   through the air
tie   to put rope round something to hold it
trial   the time when judges and other people find out what
   happened and what punishment bad people must have
untie   the opposite of 'to tie'
wave   a line of water which moves across the top of the sea
welcome   a word you say when you are pleased to see someone
wet   not dry; with water on it
wind *(n)*   the air when it moves
wood   pieces of a dead tree
worry *(v)*   to feel that something bad is going to happen
worried   unhappy and afraid

Mutiny on the Bounty

ACTIVITIES

Before Reading

1 **Read the story introduction on the first page of the book, and the back cover. How much do you know now about the story? Tick one box for each sentence.**

	YES	NO
1 The *Bounty* is a sailing ship.	☐	☐
2 The men on the ship have an easy life.	☐	☐
3 The captain's name is Fletcher Christian.	☐	☐
4 The sailors on the *Bounty* like their captain.	☐	☐
5 The sailors on the *Bounty* like Tahiti.	☐	☐
6 Tahiti is a long way from England.	☐	☐
7 The mutiny happened in 1789 near Tahiti.	☐	☐
8 The *Bounty* came home to England a year later.	☐	☐

2 **What happens in this story? Can you guess? Tick one box for each sentence.**

	YES	NO
1 The sailors kill Captain Bligh.	☐	☐
2 Fletcher Christian is the new captain.	☐	☐
3 Captain Bligh dies on the way home.	☐	☐
4 Some of the sailors stay in the south seas.	☐	☐
5 Some of the sailors marry Tahitian women.	☐	☐
6 Fletcher Christian lives to be an old man.	☐	☐

ACTIVITIES

While Reading

Read Chapter 1, and then answer these questions.

1 When did the *Bounty* leave England?
2 How old was Peter Heywood?
3 How far was it from England to Tahiti?
4 How many sailors were there on the *Bounty*?
5 How many officers were there on the *Bounty*?
6 Who was the most important man on the ship?
7 Who was the second officer?
8 Who was Otoo?
9 What did the King of England want for Jamaica?
10 How long did the *Bounty* stay in Tahiti?

Read Chapter 2. Who said this, and to whom?

1 '. . . all you officers take my things! God damn you all!'
2 'I'm in hell . . . I must leave the ship!'
3 'Many of us are afraid of Bligh – we don't like him.'
4 'What are you doing? Let me go at once!'
5 'This is our ship now.'
6 'All of you, stay on this ship! Help me, now!'
7 'Do that again, . . . and you're a dead man!'
8 'I'm thinking about Tahiti, and those beautiful women!'
9 'I'm going to live and die in hell.'

Before you read Chapter 3, can you guess what happens? Choose some endings for this sentence (you can choose as many as you like).

Captain Bligh and his eighteen men . . .

1 sail to England in the launch.   5 drink rain water.
2 sail a very long way.   6 catch birds to eat.
3 have good weather.   7 fight about the food.
4 are always hungry.   8 die in the sea.

Read Chapter 3. Here are some untrue sentences about it. Change them into true sentences.

1 From Tafua to Timor was about three thousand kilometres and it took them sixty-one days to get there.
2 At Tafua the islanders killed three men with knives.
3 When it rained, the men caught the rain water in their hands.
4 They stopped for six days on the Barrier Reef.
5 After that, it was very cold, and five men were ill.
6 Nineteen men left Tafua, but only ten arrived in Timor.

Read Chapter 4. Choose the best question-words for these questions, and then answer them.

What / Who / Why

1 . . . did the English do when they heard about the mutiny?
2 . . . came out to the *Pandora* in a canoe?
3 . . . did Christian and the others leave Toobouai?

4 . . . had a Tahitian wife called Peggy?

5 . . . did Captain Edwards do with his prisoners?

6 . . . did the *Pandora* sink?

7 . . . couldn't Stewart and four other prisoners swim?

8 . . . was the punishment for mutiny?

Before you read Chapter 5, can you guess what happens? Choose T (true) or F (false) for these sentences.

1 Peter Heywood gets the death punishment. T/F

2 Captain Bligh and Christian meet again. T/F

3 Nobody ever finds the *Bounty*. T/F

4 Christian and John Adams come back to England. T/F

5 Christian is always worried and afraid. T/F

6 John Adams lives a long and happy life. T/F

Read Chapter 5. How many true sentences can you make from this table?

Fletcher Christian John Adams Peter Heywood Captain Bligh	went to Pitcairn Island. went back to Tahiti. was a ship's captain for many years. had a son called Thursday. lived for a long time. took a Tahitian man's wife. had a lot of wives.

After Reading

1 **When Captain Bligh got home to England, the nine captains asked him many questions. Match Bligh's answers to the right questions.**

THE QUESTIONS

1 'When did the mutiny happen, Mr Bligh?'
2 'And where was your ship on that date?'
3 'Who began the mutiny?'
4 'And what did Mr Christian do?'
5 'How many other men were in the mutiny?'
6 'What did they do next, Mr Bligh?'
7 'Did they give you any food and water?'
8 'And how did you get back to England?'

CAPTAIN BLIGH'S ANSWERS

9 'Mr Fletcher Christian, my second officer.'
10 'They put me in the ship's launch, with eighteen men.'
11 'On the night of 26th April last year.'
12 'I sailed to Timor, 7,000 kilometres in an open boat, and then a Dutch ship brought us home.'
13 'There were about twelve men with guns and swords.'
14 'About twenty kilometres from the island of Tafua.'
15 'Yes, a barrel of water, and some bread and meat.'
16 'He tied my arms with a rope and took me up on deck.'

2 What happened to the men in the mutiny? Complete this passage about them with these linking words.

and / and / because / but / but / so / when / when

After the mutiny a lot of the men wanted to stay in Tahiti, _____ Christian was afraid _____ wanted to move on. He sailed to Toobouai, _____ the islanders there were not friendly, _____ he and his men sailed back to Tahiti, and then to Pitcairn Island. _____ they landed there, they burned the *Bounty*. Life was not easy on Pitcairn _____ the Tahitian men didn't like the English sailors, _____ in the end they killed most of them. The only Englishman still alive _____ the *Briton* and the *Tagus* came to Pitcairn was John Adams.

3 Here are some sentences from three diaries. Who wrote them, and when? Where were the writers at the time?

1 'This morning two English ships arrived. After all these years! Well, I can't run away now. Thursday can go out in the canoe and bring the captains here . . .'

2 'They're going to kill me, I know they are. I had no gun, no sword – I couldn't do anything! And I was only fourteen then. But they don't listen to me . . .'

3 'I'm going to do it tonight. There's moonlight, and the sea is quiet. I'm a strong swimmer, and I can rest on my piece of wood. I must get away from this hell . . .'

4 Can you find the 25 words from the story hidden in this word search? They go from left to right, and from top to bottom (4 of them are plural words).

K	B	M	C	I	Q	W	E	A	T	H	E	R	P
I	S	L	A	N	D	I	A	J	B	T	F	I	U
L	O	A	P	O	A	N	S	T	O	R	M	C	N
O	U	N	T	R	L	D	T	E	L	I	U	O	I
M	T	D	A	T	I	B	M	B	A	A	T	C	S
E	H	W	I	H	V	L	R	I	U	L	I	O	H
T	C	A	N	O	E	O	O	R	N	D	N	N	M
R	R	V	A	H	V	O	P	D	C	A	Y	U	E
E	D	E	C	K	U	D	E	S	H	I	P	T	N
S	N	S	O	F	F	I	C	E	R	W	E	S	T

5 Here are some notes from Captain Bligh's diary. Complete them with the verbs below, and 15 of the words from the word search above.

are, caught, find, found, giving, is, sailing, sink, sleep, went

15TH MAY 1789

Last night there was a big _____ and we were all afraid. The _____ was very strong and the _____ were five metres high. A lot of water came into the _____, but it didn't _____ because we used the empty _____ to throw the water back into the sea. No one could _____, so we are all tired today.

50

26TH MAY 1789

To get to Timor, we need to sail _____, but sometimes that's difficult. We're _____ about 150 _____ every day – I know that because of my _____ with knots in it. Yesterday we saw _____ for the first time – we _____ and ate three of them. So I know we _____ near _____.

6TH JUNE 1789

We _____ a way through the Barrier Reef and stopped at an _____. After six days we _____ to sea again – we must get to Timor and _____ a Dutch _____ to take us home. The _____ is hot, and two of the men are ill – I'm _____ them rum and the _____ of birds. Everybody _____ very tired, but I'm going to get all these men home, _____ and well!

6 **What do you think about the people in this story? Do you agree (A) or disagree (D) with these sentences? Say why.**

1 Bligh was a good sailor, and a good captain, because his men had good food, did not get ill, and stayed alive.

2 Bligh was a bad captain, because he was often angry; his men were afraid of him and it was not a happy ship.

3 Fletcher Christian was a better man than Captain Bligh.

4 Christian, Adams and the others were right to mutiny.

5 The sailors mutinied, not because of Captain Bligh, but because they didn't want to leave the easy life on Tahiti.

6 After the mutiny, the men were happy.

ABOUT THE AUTHOR

Tim Vicary is an experienced teacher and writer, and has written several stories for the Oxford Bookworms Library. Most of these are in the Thriller & Adventure series, including *White Death* (at Stage 1), or in the True Stories series, such as *The Coldest Place on Earth* (also at Stage 1), which tells the story of Scott's and Amundsen's race to the South Pole.

Tim Vicary has two children, and keeps dogs, cats, and horses. He lives and works in York, in the north of England, and has also published two long novels, *The Blood upon the Rose* and *Cat and Mouse*. He now lives in the country, but when he was younger, he enjoyed sailing very much. He never went as far as the Pacific islands, but he has always been interested in the story of the *Bounty* because there are so many questions about it. Why did the mutiny happen? Bligh and Christian were friends before the voyage, and Bligh was a good captain. What was Fletcher Christian really like? And what *did* happen on Pitcairn Island? Did Adams kill all the other sailors? Did the Tahitian women kill them? Nobody knows the answers to these questions.

OXFORD BOOKWORMS LIBRARY

Classics • Crime & Mystery • Factfiles • Fantasy & Horror
Human Interest • Playscripts • Thriller & Adventure
True Stories • World Stories

The OXFORD BOOKWORMS LIBRARY provides enjoyable reading in English, with a wide range of classic and modern fiction, non-fiction, and plays. It includes original and adapted texts in seven carefully graded language stages, which take learners from beginner to advanced level. An overview is given on the next pages.

All Stage 1 titles are available as audio recordings, as well as over eighty other titles from Starter to Stage 6. All Starters and many titles at Stages 1 to 4 are specially recommended for younger learners. Every Bookworm is illustrated, and Starters and Factfiles have full-colour illustrations.

The OXFORD BOOKWORMS LIBRARY also offers extensive support. Each book contains an introduction to the story, notes about the author, a glossary, and activities. Additional resources include tests and worksheets, and answers for these and for the activities in the books. There is advice on running a class library, using audio recordings, and the many ways of using Oxford Bookworms in reading programmes. Resource materials are available on the website <www.oup.com/bookworms>.

The *Oxford Bookworms Collection* is a series for advanced learners. It consists of volumes of short stories by well-known authors, both classic and modern. Texts are not abridged or adapted in any way, but carefully selected to be accessible to the advanced student.

You can find details and a full list of titles in the *Oxford Bookworms Library Catalogue* and *Oxford English Language Teaching Catalogues*, and on the website <www.oup.com/bookworms>.

THE OXFORD BOOKWORMS LIBRARY
GRADING AND SAMPLE EXTRACTS

STARTER • 250 HEADWORDS

present simple – present continuous – imperative –
can/cannot, must – *going to* (future) – simple gerunds …

Her phone is ringing – but where is it?

Sally gets out of bed and looks in her bag. No phone. She looks under the bed. No phone. Then she looks behind the door. There is her phone. Sally picks up her phone and answers it. *Sally's Phone*

STAGE 1 • 400 HEADWORDS

… past simple – coordination with *and*, *but*, *or* –
subordination with *before*, *after*, *when*, *because*, *so* …

I knew him in Persia. He was a famous builder and I worked with him there. For a time I was his friend, but not for long. When he came to Paris, I came after him – I wanted to watch him. He was a very clever, very dangerous man. *The Phantom of the Opera*

STAGE 2 • 700 HEADWORDS

… present perfect – *will* (future) – *(don't) have to, must not, could* –
comparison of adjectives – simple *if* clauses – past continuous –
tag questions – *ask/tell* + infinitive …

While I was writing these words in my diary, I decided what to do. I must try to escape. I shall try to get down the wall outside. The window is high above the ground, but I have to try. I shall take some of the gold with me – if I escape, perhaps it will be helpful later. *Dracula*

... should, may – present perfect continuous – *used to* – past perfect –
causative – relative clauses – indirect statements ...

Of course, it was most important that no one should see
Colin, Mary, or Dickon entering the secret garden. So Colin
gave orders to the gardeners that they must all keep away
from that part of the garden in future. *The Secret Garden*

STAGE 4 • 1400 HEADWORDS

... past perfect continuous – passive (simple forms) –
would conditional clauses – indirect questions –
relatives with *where/when* – gerunds after prepositions/phrases ...

I was glad. Now Hyde could not show his face to the world
again. If he did, every honest man in London would be proud
to report him to the police. *Dr Jekyll and Mr Hyde*

STAGE 5 • 1800 HEADWORDS

... future continuous – future perfect –
passive (modals, continuous forms) –
would have conditional clauses – modals + perfect infinitive ...

If he had spoken Estella's name, I would have hit him. I was so
angry with him, and so depressed about my future, that I could
not eat the breakfast. Instead I went straight to the old house.
Great Expectations

STAGE 6 • 2500 HEADWORDS

... passive (infinitives, gerunds) – advanced modal meanings –
clauses of concession, condition

When I stepped up to the piano, I was confident. It was as if I
knew that the prodigy side of me really did exist. And when I
started to play, I was so caught up in how lovely I looked that
I didn't worry how I would sound. *The Joy Luck Club*

Ned Kelly: A True Story

CHRISTINE LINDOP

When he was a boy, he was poor and hungry. When he was a young man, he was still poor and still hungry. He learnt how to steal horses, he learnt how to fight, he learnt how to live – outside the law. Australia in the 1870s was a hard, wild place. Rich people had land, poor people didn't. So the rich got richer, and the poor stayed poor.

Some say Ned Kelly was a bad man. Some say he was a good man but the law was bad. This is the true story of Australia's most famous outlaw.

The Omega Files – Short Stories

JENNIFER BASSETT

In EDI (the European Department of Intelligence in Brussels) there are some very secret files – the Omega Files. There are strange, surprising, and sometimes horrible stories in these files, but not many people know about them. You never read about them in the newspapers.

Hawker and Jude know all about the Omega Files, because they work for EDI. They think fast, they move fast, and they learn some very strange things. They go all over the world, asking difficult questions in dangerous places, but they don't always find the answers . . .